Humans have looked to the animal world for inspiration and guidance throughout the ages. By observing animals' unique attributes and behaviors, humans have uncovered valuable lessons and metaphors for life's challenges and triumphs. The animal kingdom, with its captivating array of creatures, has offered wisdom and guidance to individuals from different walks of life. Humans have found a powerful mirror for self-reflection and personal growth by looking to animals as symbols of wisdom and strength.

Enjoy coloring these fanciful images while considering each animal's contributions to providing powerful life lessons.

Aurora C. Ravenwood

Armadillo: In many spiritual beliefs, the Armadillo is seen as the keeper of boundaries. It reminds us of the importance of setting healthy boundaries and teaches protection and shielding oneself from harm. It's also associated with introspection and solitude due to its solitary nature.

Bear: Bears are power animals symbolizing strength, courage, and grounding. In many cultures, the Bear is considered a symbol of introspection, inner knowledge, and dream interpretation. Bear energy helps you stand against adversity and restore harmony and balance in life.

Beaver: The Beaver represents industry, teamwork, and construction. It teaches us about the importance of fulfilling our duties for the common good, and building our dreams and goals with determination and strong foundations. It also speaks about the balance between work and play.

Bee: The Bee, in the spiritual realm, embodies harmony, productivity, and community. It represents the sweet results of hard work and perseverance, but also underscores the importance of working together and the power of communication.

Blue Jay: The Blue Jay is associated with assertiveness, intelligence, and vibrancy. They symbolize the power of the voice and the importance of communication and speaking one's truth. They are also seen as protectors of family and community.

Buffalo: The Buffalo symbolizes abundance, survival, and gratitude. It teaches us to value our resources and reminds us of the sacredness of life. Buffalo energy brings strength, endurance, and provision.

Butterfly: The Butterfly is a powerful symbol of transformation, lightness, and beauty. It represents profound changes of the soul and the potential for personal growth. Its emergence from the chrysalis signifies hope, rebirth, and metamorphosis.

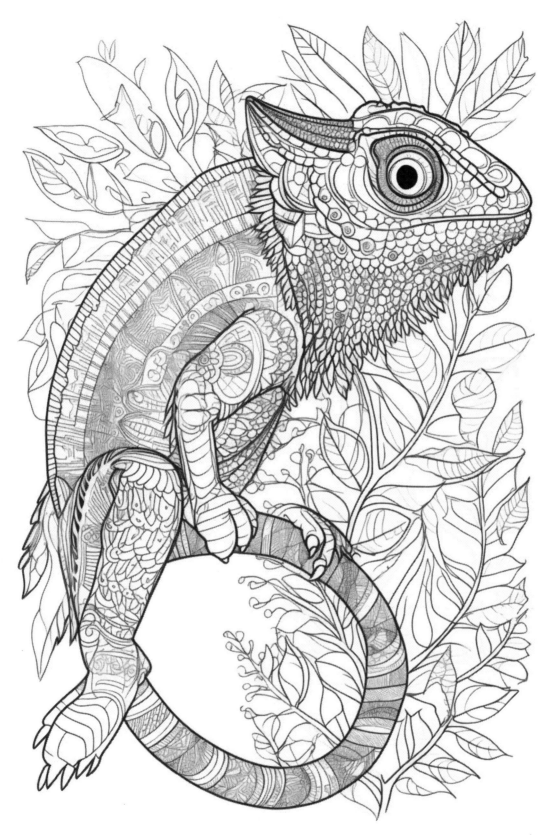

Chameleon: The Chameleon signifies adaptability, patience, and invisibility. Its ability to change color represents blending in and adapting to situations, while its patience while hunting is a lesson in waiting for the right moment to act.

Cheetah: The cheetah is associated with speed, focus, and self-esteem. It embodies quick decision making, swift action, and the ability to stay focused on goals despite obstacles. Cheetah energy inspires personal power and the pursuit of one's ambitions.

Chipmunk: The Chipmunk represents curiosity, playfulness, and preparation. It teaches us to balance work and play, and encourages us to prepare for the future while still enjoying the present.

Crow: The Crow symbolizes magic, mystery, and transformation. It represents the universal law of truth and is believed to be a guide between the physical and spiritual realms. Crow's wisdom encourages us to see beyond the limitations of human perception.

Deer: Deer embodies gentleness, grace, and compassion. As a guide, it teaches kindness, peacefulness, and the ability to listen. Deer energy urges us to be gentle with ourselves and others, and to foster deep connections with our surroundings.

Dolphin: The Dolphin symbolizes joy, playfulness, and intelligence. They are known to represent harmony and balance and encourage communication and companionship. Dolphin energy can guide us to rediscover our inner joy and to live in harmony with others.

Donkey: Donkeys are associated with humility, patience, and hard work. They symbolize the endurance and determination required to carry heavy burdens, urging us to remain steadfast during difficult times

Dragonfly: The Dragonfly symbolizes transformation, adaptability, and the realm of emotions. It invites us to explore our emotions and illusions and encourages us to seek change and self-realization.

Eagle: The Eagle represents spiritual enlightenment, freedom, and courage. It's seen as a messenger from the divine, symbolizing perspective and the ability to see the bigger picture. Eagle energy encourages us to soar above life's challenges with grace and resilience.

Elephant: Elephants signify strength, wisdom, and loyalty. Their long memory symbolizes the importance of history and learning from the past. Elephant energy provides us with the determination to overcome obstacles, the wisdom to understand the world, and the loyalty to stay true to our communities.

Fox: The Fox symbolizes cleverness, adaptability, and invisibility. It represents the ability to see through deception and make wise decisions. Fox energy reminds us to be observant, swift, and cunning in our dealings

Frog: Frogs are associated with cleansing, rebirth, and transformation. The Frog represents the journey of transitioning from one phase to another and encourages us to leap forward into new opportunities with a clean slate.

Goat: The Goat symbolizes ambition, determination, and sure-footedness. They are the embodiments of perseverance and teach us to stay determined even when the path gets tough.

Horse: Horses are symbols of power, freedom, and travel. As a spiritual guide, the Horse urges us to harness our personal power, seek our freedom, and journey with courage

Hummingbird: The Hummingbird is associated with joy, lightness, and resilience. It embodies the ability to endure long journeys despite its small size, teaching us that even the smallest of things can possess great strength and endurance.

Jaguar: The Jaguar signifies stealth, power, and the mystery of the unknown. It's a symbol of rebirth and the power to face our fears. Jaguar energy encourages us to explore the shadows and confront our deepest fears.

Manatee: Manatees are associated with gentleness, kindness, and calmness. They teach us to navigate emotional waters with grace and to approach life's challenges with a sense of peace and tranquility.

Mouse: The Mouse represents attention to detail, resourcefulness, and adaptability. Its ability to thrive in a variety of environments teaches us to adapt to change and appreciate the small details in life.

Ostrich: The Ostrich signifies practicality, grounding, and truth. It encourages us to keep our feet on the ground, deal with problems head-on, and not to avoid reality.

Otter: Otters are symbols of playfulness, creativity, and balance. They teach us to balance work and play and to foster a sense of community and cooperation.

Owl: The Owl is a symbol of wisdom, intuition, and the ability to see what others do not. As a spiritual guide, it teaches us to trust our intuition, explore the unknown, and seek wisdom in the darkness.

Panda: Pandas are associated with tranquility, gentleness, and balance. They teach us to lead a balanced life, reminding us that despite life's challenges, we must always find time for relaxation and tranquility.

Pangolin: The Pangolin represents protection, self-care, and introspection. Its ability to curl up into a ball teaches us to protect ourselves when needed, and its solitary nature reminds us of the importance of self-care and reflection.

Parrot: Parrots are symbols of communication, vibrancy, and exposure. They teach us to express our feelings effectively, embrace our own uniqueness, and not to fear being in the spotlight.

Peacock: The Peacock stands for beauty, self-expression, and immortality. It encourages us to show our true colors and be proud of who we are. Peacock energy reminds us to strive for self-awareness and inner beauty.

Penguin: Penguins symbolize community, adaptability, and endurance. They teach us to adapt to harsh conditions, to cooperate with others, and to stay resilient in the face of adversity.

Polar Bear: The Polar Bear is associated with strength, survival, and solitude. It symbolizes the power to thrive in solitude and the wisdom and strength to survive in harsh environments.

Rabbit: Rabbits represent abundance, creativity, and vulnerability. The Rabbit encourages us to multiply our efforts, be creative in our pursuits, and to understand the power within our vulnerabilities.

Raccoon: Raccoons are associated with curiosity, resourcefulness, and adaptability. They encourage us to explore our surroundings, make use of available resources, and adapt to changes with ease.

Ram: The Ram represents determination, action, and leadership. Its energy is of assertiveness, helping us to take charge of our life, push forward in adversity, and to lead by example.

Raven: The Raven stands for transformation, mystery, and magic. It's often seen as a messenger between realms and embodies the profound transformation of the soul. Raven energy guides us to embrace change and dive into the unknown.

Rhinoceros: Rhinoceroses symbolize peace, stability, and assurance. They teach us to be comfortable in our own skin, promoting a sense of self-assurance and tranquility in the face of adversity.

Rooster: The Rooster is associated with confidence, vigilance, and resurrection. It signifies the ability to rise with every fall and to stand tall with confidence, reminding us to always be observant and resilient.

Seahorse: Seahorses represent patience, perspective, and generosity. Their unique parenting style, where the male carries the eggs, teaches us about equality and sharing responsibilities.

Sea lion: Sea lions symbolize playfulness, joy, and balance. They encourage us to find a balance between our responsibilities and our need for joy and relaxation.

Shark: The Shark stands for survival, adaptability, and instinct. Its power teaches us about survival instinct, the need to adapt to changes quickly, and to trust our instincts.

Sheep: Sheep are associated with innocence, gentleness, and collective consciousness. They teach us about the power of community, the importance of peace, and the innocence that comes from trusting in the collective.

Snake: The Snake is a symbol of transformation, healing, and life force. Its shedding skin signifies rebirth and renewal. Snake energy encourages us to embrace change, seek healing, and tap into the primal life force within us.

Squirrel: Squirrels represent preparation, activity, and adaptability. They teach us about the importance of preparation, the need for activity and movement, and the ability to adapt to different situations.

Swan: Swans are symbols of grace, beauty, and transformation. They teach us to embrace our inner beauty, navigate life with grace, and to embrace personal transformation.

Tiger: The Tiger signifies power, passion, and sensuality. As a spiritual guide, it encourages us to embrace our power, channel our passions, and to explore the sensual aspects of our nature.

Toucan: Toucans are associated with communication, self-expression, and showmanship. They encourage us to express ourselves freely, speak our truth, and to be unafraid of standing out from the crowd.

Walrus: Walruses represent protection, adaptation, and survival. They remind us to protect ourselves and those we love, to adapt to our surroundings, and to endure the toughest conditions.

Wolf: Wolves symbolize instinct, freedom, and social connections. They teach us to trust our instincts, value our freedom, and to understand the importance of strong social connections.

Made in the USA
Middletown, DE
16 October 2023

40653423R00057